Mosaic Of Moments

Embrace Change, Embrace Life

ANINDITA LAHIRI BISWAS

India | USA | UK

Made with ❤ on the BookLeaf Publishing Platform
www.bookleafpub.in
www.bookleafpub.com

Dedication

This book is dedicated to the four pillars of my strength:
To my beloved husband, the Mr.Sudeep Biswas, whose love was the light in my darkest hours.
To my mother, Muchhanda Lahiri, whose unwavering support and wisdom kept me grounded.
To my younger brother Pinaki Lahiri, whose boundless energy and belief in me never wavered.
To my sister-in-law Madhavi Lahiri, whose love, affection, care and inspiring words helped me fight out the critical situation peacefully. It is because of all of you that I found the courage to battle the deadly monstrous cancer in 2022.

Your love, your presence, and your strength were my constant fuel. Each page of this book echoes your sacrifices, your patience, and your faith in me.
Without you, these 50 poems would not exist,
For you taught me resilience, the power of family, and the gift of never giving up.
This collection is a testament to the fight we fought together,
And to the love that continues to carry me forward.
In your memory, I write. In your honour, I live.

Preface

Dear poetry enthusiasts,

Education is not just a profession for me; it is a lifelong passion that has shaped my identity and purpose. With over 25 years of experience as a science educator in reputed schools, I have had the privilege of guiding countless young minds toward knowledge and curiosity. Teaching has always been my calling, deeply ingrained in me through generations—my maternal grandparents were educators, and I believe this noble profession runs in my blood. From my childhood, I was sincere and hardworking, with good academic records and interest in various fields like debate, essay writing, athletics, painting etc. My father was a paper technologist, who worked in various paper factories all over India and my mother is a dedicated homemaker. As we used to move with my father, my younger brother and I studied in different cities in India.

My late husband, **Mr. Sudeep Biswas** and I, stayed in Jaipur. I worked as a middle school science HOD for 12 years till march 2022. I lost my beloved husband to COVID in July 2021, in Jaipur. In July 2021, I relocated to Pune to stay with my mother, now being single, and continued to work online for my school in Jaipur. Following my diagnosis of cancer in March of 2022, I resigned. The fight against the deadly monstrous cancer started with numerous chemo-therapies and surgeries. The road was dark and very stormy, but I could sail through as I was lucky enough to get treated by best of doctors, love, care and support from family members and financial help provided by various educational organisations, where I was working at that time. This boosted my confidence and helped in my treatment. I never felt abandoned in the fight as I am blessed to have friends who are my extended family members. They kept visiting and calling me only to bring a smile on my face, keeping my spirits high.

My Principal from JPHS in Jaipur, **Mrs. Madhu Maini**, is my mentor and guide, whose affectionate and caring words over phone and texts, boosted my morale during the darkest days of my treatment. It's her appreciation for my poems that fuelled my zeal for writing. This book is the outcome of all the appreciation and interest she showed in my compositions in spite of her extremely busy schedule. I would like to take a moment to express my heartfelt gratitude for Madhu ma'am's guidance, support and cooperation during my tenure in Jayshree Periwal High School, Jaipur.

I earned my living during my 2 years of treatment by taking online classes with an ed-tech company, Byjus. It was possible to work for me as they empathised with me, understanding the way I was handling the tough situation alone, being a single woman. This made getting leaves for hospitalisation a pleasant breeze. I would like to express my heartfelt gratitude to Byjus' reporting mangers, **Ms. Sanjita Shukla** and **Mr. Krishnag Kumar Singh**, who were kind souls, understanding and emphathising with me to reschedule my sessions immediately so that I can complete my treatment without stress. They took initiative to collect funds from the Byjus' team for my treatment and deposited it in my account. They did it voluntarily and I was unaware that such great and timely help can come from an organisation which I had joined on the 1st Jan, 2022. I was moved to my core by their humanitarian gesture and I am forever grateful to them for the help they rendered in my toughest days.

It was during the pandemic times I started to pen down the thoughts that poured straight from my heart. The first few poems were written to spread awareness about COVID and wearing a mask. My first poem, 'Awareness', getting published in the Times NIE on the 16th of May 2021, catapulted me on my journey as a modern-day poet. Consequently, when I started getting hospitalised for chemotherapy cycles and surgeries, I kept writing poems from my hospital bed on whatever topics came to mind as a way to keep myself busy, using creative expression to divert my attention from the disease I was battling. Many of my loved ones suggested that the time has come to compile all those verses into a book of poetry to reach more readers. This gave birth to my beloved brainchild, 'Mosaic Of Moments', which contains verses on embracing changes and embracing life. My intent to publish these verses is to ignite, inspire and impact my dear readers to find creative ways to battle their demons.

My message to all my readers is – Fight every challenging situation that life throws at you bravely, by building your mental strength and believing in yourself. As to be alive and not just live, one needs to face the challenges with a positive mind, only then can you manage to live better in the present.

As Master Oogway said, "Yesterday is history, tomorrow is a mystery, but today is a gift. That is why it is called the present." (Kung Fu Panda).

With love and gratitude,
Anindita Lahiri Biswas

Acknowledgements

As I pen down my first collection of poetry, **"Mosaic Of Moments"**, I would like to take a moment to express my heartfelt gratitude to the individuals whose love, support, and encouragement have been the pillars of my strength during some of the most challenging moments of my life.

First and foremost, I owe everything to my family. My mother has been a constant source of love and care. Her strength and grace have been a beacon of inspiration. I am deeply grateful to my younger brother, his wife, and my niece for their unwavering support during my battle with cancer. They ensured that my needs were met, and more importantly, they kept me stress-free, which played a crucial role in my healing journey.

A special thanks to my sister-in-law, **Sushmita Debroy**, who reached out to me every single day, showing genuine concern for my health. Her thoughtful conversations on various topics uplifted my spirits and kept me positive throughout this process. I am equally thankful to my father-in-law, **Satyendranath Biswas**, who, stood by my side with his silent prayers and profound wisdom, guiding me towards the light at the end of the dark tunnel.

I am also blessed with the friendship and support of my childhood friends and workplace colleagues, including **Babita Pujari,Smita Ghatge, Sabitha Varma, Meghna Kuthe, Geeta Bharre, Shina Jaimon, Rajni Dudhe Sonali Dudhane, Madhavi Athale, Archana Hivelekar, Anuradha Rao, Priti Sharma, Varsha Kokil, Mrinalini Bhosale, Reena Kapoor, Anand Jaju, Shakil Kunju, Anagha Tol, and Devendra Bannagade**. Despite their busy lives and the distance they had to travel from outside Pune, few of them continually kept in touch by calling me and rest of them visited me, ensuring that my spirits remained high.

Lastly, I would like to extend my deepest gratitude to a very special young friend, **Master Sasmit Lahiri**. Though we share the same surname, we are not related by blood. Sasmit was once my science student in grade 7 at JPHS, Jaipur, in April 2020. For four long years, he sent me messages of encouragement, wishing me well on my road to recovery. His unwavering support, along with his appreciation for my poetry, inspired me to bring forth this book into the world.

I extend heartfelt thanks to **Mrinalini Fernandes**, M.A., B.Ed, Principal of Vikhe Patil Memorial School, Pune —A visionary educationist and true leader, inspiring by example and action. Her guidance, thoughtful feedback and unwavering support enriched my poetic voice.

My warm gratitude to **Sharvani Lahiri** — just 20 yrs, yet wise beyond her years. She is an all-rounder, a voracious reader, and a soul full of empathy and zest. Her youthful insight, keen eye, and boundless enthusiasm brought fresh perspective. Each of these individuals has contributed to my journey, both in the realm of recovery and creativity. Without their love and encouragement, **'Mosaic Of Moments'** would not have been possible. From the bottom of my heart, I thank you all for being part of my story.

With love and gratitude,
Anindita Lahiri Biswas

1. Foreword

Dear readers,

In the face of adversity, some people find solace in silence, while others find their voice in the midst of turmoil. For our blossoming poetess, Anindita Lahiri Biswas, the battle with cancer became a crucible of creativity, as she poured her heart and soul into these poems. Written over 33 sessions of chemotherapy and countless hours of hospitalization, these verses are a testament to the human spirit's capacity for resilience, hope, and transformation.

Through her words, we witness Anindita's journey from darkness to light, from fear to acceptance, and from pain to peace. With each poem, we are invited to walk alongside her, to share in her struggles, and to find solace in the knowledge that we are not alone in our own battles.

These poems are not just a reflection of her personal experience, but a celebration of the human condition in all its complexity and beauty. They speak to the fragility and strength of life, the power of love and connection, and the indomitable will to survive and thrive.

As you read these poems, may you find comfort, inspiration, and a deeper understanding of the excruciating experiences that a frightening illness can bring. May these words be a balm to your soul, a reminder that even in the darkest moments, there is always hope, and that the light of creativity and love can pierce even the most profound darkness.

With Love
Mrinalini Fernandes
Vikhe Patil Memorial School, Pune
Principal

2. Foreword

Dear readers,

I am honored to write this foreword for Anindita Lahiri Biswas's captivating collection of poems, " Mosaic Of Moments ". As a college friend, I have had the privilege of witnessing Anindita's growth as a poet and a person. Anindita's poetry is nectar of her journey with fighting cancer. With each poem, she invites us to reflect and feel the world around us. What strikes me most about Anindita's poetry is that it resonates with your feelings, her ability to highlight the simplest emotions honestly. Her resilient attitude through the toughest times has bestowed upon her a deep understanding of life which manifests in her poetry. These three decades of my friendship with Anindita and witnessing her growth as a person and poet is a blessing. Her poems have a way of evoking emotions, sparking thoughts that linger on long after you finish reading. In the book "Mosaic Of Moments ", Anindita shares her gift with us, offering a glimpse into her emotional core. I am confident that readers will find inspiration and the light at the end of the tunnel from her poems that sing about her hardships and successes. Congratulations, Anindita on this remarkable achievement. I am proud to be your friend.

Sincerely,
Lt Colonel Sonali Dudhane (Retd)

1. Awareness

The invisible virus
Had taken all of us again to task
So don't forget to wear a mask
If you want to tide over the pandemic fast.
Follow the set norms till the last.
As you want to live longer, it's a must.

Wearing a mask while stepping out is obligatory,
Social distancing is compulsory.
Saying no to partying is not derogatory.
Saying no to celebration should not be offensive
That's how one can be defensive.
Also do not share your Tiffin
To escape entry into the coffin
Bake at home yummy muffin...

As sharing is no more caring
'Be positive' is no more good word
Going out to work to help the nation
Is no more the right notion.

Only step out to get your ration.
Stay indoors to help your nation.
Or else lock down is the only option.
To contain the spread of infection.
Take proper precautions,
to keep away the tension.

The present situation may bring depression,
Try to tide over it by creative expression
Stay connected using internet communication
Where friends pep up each other through appreciation.

This is not a year to calculate loss or profit
Instead thank God if you are staying fit.
Remember that the whole world is pandemic hit.
Salute the doctors in PPE kit

Quarantine is not pristine
Herd immunity was never earlier heard.
Asymptomatic is very traumatic

So each one of us should take care of ourselves,
Nation will be taken care of automatically!
(Written in March 2021 during the pandemic times)

2. Virtual Learning

The academic session was virtual,
But the learning was perpetual.
Making us all habitual,
To tackle the unforeseen.

Left Children with no option.
Inspite of internet interruption,
They exhibited cooperation,
And lived up to our expectations.

This was all possible,
As Our school was responsible,
So that we are not susceptible,
Working hours were flexible.

They were quick in vaccination,
To help in country's immunisation,
Controlling virus transmission.

Many Lost jobs, some lost dear one's,

But still the show must go on.
Keeping in mind,
Let's be kind.

There is uncertainty looming
But keep your positivity blooming
Nothing in this world is permanent
So have right temperament.

Without doubting your capabilities.
Convert challenges into opportunities.
Making best out of your abilities.

Pause a while to cherish good times
Never give up self-confidence at difficult time.
Keep faith in God at all times!
(Written in November 2020,when I taught my school
students virtually.)

3. A Teacher

The year that has gone,
Will be remembered by everyone.
The path was rough,
The times were tough,
Scope to rest was not enough.

But with teaching as our passion,
We marched towards our mission
Embracing the new tools of digitisation.
So that kids get the motivation,
To give wings to their imagination.

Fulfilling everybody's expectations,
Without portraying our real situations.
Realising that each one has their limitation
But still trying to reach perfection
With our leader's inspiration.....
We reached the end of this academic session.

With the same zeal and motivation

We are starting the new academic session
Come March end with Teachers Orientation
A yet another beginning of
'May be' a hybrid session

Who are we.....?
We are God's creation
Building great Nation
.....A proud TEACHER

4. Born To Impress

Dress up to impress, with style and flair,
Speak your heart out, and let your true self share,
Go shopping when you're feeling down, and need a pick-
me-up,
Relax a while when life gets tough, and you're feeling
hard-pressed.

Don't let societal norms suppress or oppress you,
Set your own rules, and be the queen of your own
kingdom, it's true,
You're born to be an empress, with a spirit that's free,
So rule your world with confidence, and let your
personality shine with glee.

5. An Extra Day

A little extra day of the year,
A little extra time.
An extra opportunity to do little more.

To love more
To celebrate more
To create more memories

So leap into the future
With renewed hope anew,
With enthusiasm that shines right through.
Make the most of this bonus day's might,
And turn it into a brighter, bolder light.

6. Let's Celebrate

Let's celebrate the life we've got.
Let's relish our food while it's hot.
Let's use the resources we take,
Let's keep the promises we make.

Let's exchange the ideas we get,
Let's reach the goals we set.
Let's enjoy the present moment,
Let's create a healthy environment.

Let's learn to smile in every situation,
Let's help build a strong nation.
Let's communicate our feelings,
Let's be transparent in our dealings.

Let's cross the hurdles we face,
Let's learn to understand the people we embrace.
Let's break the barriers created by caste, creed, and
nationality,
Let's practice humanity.

Let's learn to appreciate each other more,
Let's understand our mother nature to the core.
Let's learn to face sunshine and rain,
Let's practice something rare, using our brains.

Let's take pride in our own traditions,
Let's respect others' opinions.
Let's use our time to learn new skills,
So that in times to come, we can chill.

7. Journey

If the road in front of you is dark,
Light it up with your spark.
Leave behind an indelible mark,
Transform with love those who nark.
Have a heart where kindness parks,
There will be many on the path to bark.
Even if it's stormy, embark
To set out on a journey, in search of a landmark

8. Nature

When I see winged creatures with their wings open,
ready to take flight, it lifts my energies,
and I wait for them to sing.
The twinkling light of the stars at night
is soothing to my soul,
and I am humbled by
the vastness of the universe.

A flowering plant laden with pink blooms,
dancing with the gentle,
cool breeze right under my balcony,
reminds me of the rhythm in nature.
The soft, cottony clouds drifting through the clear sky
keep me moving along with them.

Thus, nature's beauty is everywhere, mesmerizing, isn't
it?
One just needs to stand and stare up!

9. A Hand

A hand is the best tool for humans. So let your hand be:

A hand that helps others,
A hand that nurses the sick,
A hand that folds in prayer,
A hand that supports weak and frail senior citizens,

A hand that claps at others' success,
A hand that nurtures the growth of a baby,
A hand that fixes problems,
A hand that loves to give to those in need,

A hand that nurtures a seed into a tree,
A hand that builds and creates for all,
A hand that salutes the heroes of the nation,
A hand that builds a better nation,

A hand is the architect of our destiny.
The more you use it, the better it becomes.
Thus, it is a truly wonderful human organ.

10. Solace In Solitude

In solitude, a much-needed grace unfolds,
A gentle silence, a sacred space to hold.
Whispers calm the restless mind, and solace blooms,
In hearts confined, a sense of peace resumes.

Alone, yet never truly lone, for in this stillness,
We're fully known, our true selves revealed in
gentleness.
The world fades out, and in its place, a quiet fills,
A sacred space where the heart can heal and fulfill.

The noise outside may scream and roar,
But within us, something more profound is in store.
A gentle strength, a beautiful glow, emerges to guide,
Teaching us how to let go, and step aside.

In solitude, we search our way, pausing to reflect,
A chance to sway with emotions that wander, soft and
free to inspect.
A quiet connection forms between you and me,

In the emptiness, we can heal, and learn to listen, wild
and carefree.

Solace is found in peace apart, a soothing balm to the
soul,
A peaceful place that calms the weary heart, making it
whole.

11. I Am Not Just Numbers

I am not just a number, I am so much more,
A strength that overcomes my weaknesses, and a hope
that roars,
I am the undying spirit that fights against all odds,
An artist painting my canvas with colors of my own
chords.

I am not defined by age, or percent, or scores,
Nor by the marks I get, or the leaves I've taken before,
I am not to be weighed on a scale, or measured by my
height,
I stand tall in every situation, shining with my own light.

I am a story, inspiring and motivating in my own way,
A poet at heart, expressing myself, come what may,
Don't judge me by mere numbers, or units of measure,
I am not in a mad race, or competition to secure scores.

My competition is with the person I see every morning,

The one who looks back at me, with a reflection that's
warning,
Don't judge me by numbers, I am the energy to spread
light,
In the darkest of forests, I shine with all my might.

Numbers don't matter to me, I am mind over matter,
I am not to be defined by digits, or any form of chatter,
I am a unique individual, with my own strengths and
flair,
And I will not be reduced to just a number, I will rise
above with care.

12. Return Ticket

We hold a return ticket, date unknown,
Same starting point, same destination shown.
Time's short between arrival and departure's call,
Make the most of your stay, and give your all.

Travel light, and make your journey free,
Meet fellow travelers, with stories to see.
Some will delight, some will try your patience too,
But each one has a tale, and a heart that's true.

Listen well to each, with compassion and care,
Touch every soul, and show you truly share.
If you can make a difference, in just one heart's plight,
Consider yourself worthy, of this final, last light.

13. Never Thought

I never thought I'd find the strength to fight,
To bear the weight of so much pain, and still ignite,
I never thought I'd heal the wounds that wouldn't mend,
Or calm the storms that raged, and seemed to never end.

I never thought I'd rise again, after falling so many times,
But still I pushed forward, through the darkness and the
grime,
I never thought I'd reach this place, where I stand today,
But here I am, and I'm grateful for the journey's way.

And though I've lost loved ones, and felt the sting of
sorrow,
I'm thankful for the strength that's been mine to borrow,
Gratitude to the almighty, for guiding me through every
test,
And providing me with the courage to face each new
quest.

14. Move On

Some people will judge you, but don't let their words
define,
Move on, and stay true to yourself, and your own shine.
Some will hurt you, but forgiveness is the key,
To finding peace, and moving on, wild and free.

Some will love you, and show you kindness and care,
Reciprocate their love, and show them you're aware,
Thank the universe for the love that's real,
And move on, with a heart that's full and healed.

Some will motivate you, and help you grow,
Consider yourself lucky, and let their words show,
Get motivated, and take action with ease,
And move on, with a sense of purpose, and a heart that's
free.

Some will inspire you, and spark a fire within,
Take the inspiration, and let your dreams begin,
Some will complement you, and make you feel seen,

Be satisfied, feel good, and move on, with a heart that's
serene.

Some will help you, and lend a hand,
Be grateful to them, and take a stand,
Some will understand you, and see things from your
view,
Be mature enough to understand them, and move on,
with a heart that's true.

Each one of them played a role, in shaping your
personality,
So be thankful to each one, and let gratitude be your
currency,
Believe in yourself, and be yourself, that's the key,
To living a life that's authentic, and wild, and free.

15. War

Who benefits from the war?
Can't the masters behind the conflict hear
The cries of victims, near and far?
Everywhere, there's man-made suffering and unrest,
Putting humanity to the test.

People dying of thirst and poverty,
No empathy in the community,
People waiting for bread are fed with bombs,
Many babies never see the light of life beyond the womb.

An eye for an eye is not the solution,
It's turning the whole world blind,
We're blind to the misery, pain, and suffering around us,
What's the final outcome of war?

It doesn't matter who wins or who loses,
War is equally devastating for both countries,
Only innocent people and children lose their lives,
Political leaders gain from the strife.

Many children become orphans and homeless,
How can one be so heartless?
To overlook such pain and suffering is a crime,
My soul cries out in anguish.

Will I see the day when news headlines read:
"There is peace in the world?

16. Pain

When happiness surrounds you, friends and celebrations
abound,
But when pain and sorrow come, you're often left to face
it alone, in silence profound,
It's in these moments of solitude, that you discover who
truly cares,
And learn to find strength, in the midst of tears, and the
weight of your fears.

The pain of losing loved ones, never truly fades,
We never get over it, we just learn to live with the ache,
and the shades,
But it's in this pain, that we evolve, and grow, and
become,
A better version of ourselves, with a heart that's more
resilient, and a soul that's more serene.

When baked in the fire of pain, we emerge stronger, and
more refined,

Painful days may seem too long, but they teach us
patience, and acceptance, in time,
It's a better teacher, than happier experiences, that often
leave us unchanged,
For pain forces us to confront, our deepest emotions, and
to rearrange.

The heart pours out, and emotions flow, like a river's
stream,
Don't try to hold yourself back, let your feelings be seen,
Give words to your emotions, and let them take shape,
And you may find, that you've composed, the best poem
of your life, in the midst of your pain, and your ache.

17. Love For Travelling

Sometimes my mind starts wandering,
Taking me to far-off distant places,
I wonder if it can take me to where my loved ones dwell,
I pray to God to free me from the chains of disease.

I long to travel through valleys with green meadows,
Beautiful fields of flowers, birds singing in the woods,
Echoing hills, and sun rays peeping through the lovely
canopy,
I want to soak myself in nature's beauty.

Travelling, I miss you so much, as you teach me so
much,
Travelling is learning, you de-stress me to a great extent,
You give me moments to capture, and I love travelling,
As it leaves the past behind, compelling me to be in
present.

With hope to see more unknown lands and meet more
beautiful souls,

I wish I could travel soon to meet my near and dear ones,
Even as I sit here, my mind is still travelling.

31

18. Conquer The Cancer

Oh, cancer, you're not so powerful,
Just an uncontrolled growth of cells, after all,
You can be tamed with tiny chemical molecules' might,
I have faith in God, who heals, and in my doctors'
tireless fight.

My spirit will never cease, I'll conquer this disease,
I trust in the efforts of those who bring me ease,
I'm not alone in pain, there are many more who suffer
too,
But I'll maintain a grin, and see this journey through.

Lost hair will regrow, I'll regain my former might,
I believe that my pain and suffering will subside with
time and light,
Death, pain, and darkness are life's realities, it's true,
But they make us cherish moments of joy, healing, and
knowledge anew.

There's no gain without pain, no light without darkness'
shade,
Life is beautiful, but death is a journey to a new parade,
The soul sets off on another beautiful quest,
And though it's uncharted, I'll face it with courage and
rest.

19. Face The Battle

Cancer may batter the body, but it cannot break the
mind,
Nor deter the spirit, that's determined to shine.
A surge of strength rises, like a storm inside,
An urge to win over, and let resilience be your guide.

Merge with the courage, that's within your soul,
And face the battle, with a heart that's whole,
For though the body may weaken, the spirit remains
strong,
And with each challenge, your resolve grows, and your
will is long.

20. Rest In Peace

Cancer confined me to the four walls.
But I have an alert brain
Whose thoughts wander wildly?
On the mountains, in the valleys,
With the dancing waves everywhere.
I have a heart that beats
To keep enthusiasm alive.
A mind that is filled with mindfulness
Which wants to express endlessly.
A soul that constantly
Yearns to live in peace before it's too late.
Then only I can rest in peace.

21. A Cup of Tea

Tea made with a dip dip dip....
Relish its every sip

When friends meet after a long time,
They remember the fun they had in canteen during tea
time,
It's all so nostalgic,
Thus tea has power to create magic.

Tea sip matters a lot,
When it kept tightly closed in a pot,
Love every sip when it is hot.

It causes boost in our energy.
So that we are not in lethargy.
Take a sip with a friend,
You can set a trend.

Cherish tea time with your partner
In morning or after the dinner.

With your parents and relatives
It's bound to be addictive.

It may be a variety from Darjeeling or Assam
The effect it gives is awesome.

Plucked delicately and carefully by lovely ladies
From mountainous tea garden to factories.
Where tea leaves undergoes drying and disruption.
To stop the leaf enzymes cause oxidation.

Our biological clock is set for tea time
With friends and gossips over a cup of tea is fun time.

22. Our Earth, Our Home

Our Earth, our home, a beautiful blue sphere,
Nurtures every creature, like a mother, always near.
It's up to us to safeguard its future with care,
By conserving its resources, and showing we truly care.

If not, soon we'll be in tears, and our next generation will
face danger,
If we continue to satisfy our greed, the Earth will no
longer be able to range,
Our needs will go unmet, and the consequences will be
dire,
So let's take a step to sow a seed, and remove the weed
that conspires.

Protecting forests is the need of the time, indeed,
All animals have the right to food and shelter, it's a noble
deed,
We must be nature's conservators, dear friends, and take
a stand,

So we don't need to repent later, and the Earth can thrive
in this land.

Plant trees, to plant hope, and a brighter future to see,
Save Earth, to save our home, for you and me.

23. Hope For The Best

Leave your nest, spread your wings and fly,
Come out of your comfort zone, and reach for the sky,
Give up the least, and strive for the best,
Be prepared for the test, and do your utmost quest.

It's not the time to rest, or let your guard down,
Do your best to keep away the pest, and wear your
crown,
And always hope for the best, with a heart full of cheer,
And trust that your efforts will bring you success, and
banish all fear.

24. Reality

Reality is intense, a truth that's permanent and strong,
Hard to accept, yet it's a rare commodity, where we all
belong,
It lies in being present, facing life's challenges head-on,
And embracing the truth, that's often difficult to be
known.

Being real is the key, to a life that's authentic and true,
For our existence is real, and our mortality is a fact,
anew,
Being yourself is the greatest reality, that we can face,
And finding real people, with real emotions, and a real,
strong pace.

In this era of virtual reality, it's hard to find,
Real friends, real relationships, that are genuine, and
kind,
But when we do, we must hold on tight,
And cherish the connections, that bring us joy, and make
our hearts take flight.

Faking it, builds a bubble, that can burst at any time,
Leading to chaos, and a life that's messy, and hard to
redefine,
But being real, and authentic, builds a strong personality,
That's rooted in truth, and a sense of humanity.

So let's embrace reality, and be sensitive, strong, and
humane,
And find the real people, who can silence the turmoil,
and bring us peace, and calm, and a sense of being sane,
For in the end, it's the real connections, that we make,
That bring us joy, and a sense of purpose, and a life that's
authentic, and at stake.

25. I Must

I must eat, even if my taste buds are numb,
I must sleep, even if restlessness has become my plight.
I must take medicine, despite its potent might,
And keep talking, even when words feel like a fight.

I must endure the prick of needles, though it hurts,
And walk on shaky legs, with a destination that asserts,
A return to normalcy, where health and strength revive,
And the shackles of disease are broken, and freedom
thrives.

Disease may be formidable, but it's not greater than I,
I'll harness my mind's resilience, and let my body heal
and fly,
I'll process my thoughts, and shake off the weight,
And emerge stronger, with a spirit that cannot be
swayed.

26. My Sarees And I

My Sarees and I
My sarees are my greatest treasure, a joy to behold,
Taking them out of the suitcase, a pleasure that never
grows old.
The time spent maintaining them is a love affair,
With solar exposure, they stay healthy, and their beauty
is beyond compare.

My mom may say, "Give a few away,"
But I won't succumb to the pressure, no way,
My sarees and I, we have a special bond,
We converse in leisure, our own sweet beyond.

When wrapped in a saree, I feel like a queen,
Posing for photos, in different postures, serene,
It's the most graceful attire, a sight to behold,
Compelling one and all to stare, with hearts that unfold.

With love and respect for the hands that weave,
I salute the weavers, and the art they conceive,

I'll cherish the company of my sarees, always near,
A treasure trove of memories, and emotions that bring
me cheer.

27. Mathematics Of Life

Mathematics is an abstract art,
Teaching us to subtract sorrows, and multiply love and
joy from the start,
It adds knowledge to our minds, every single day,
And shows us how to divide time and care, in a way
that's fair and just, in every way.

Mathematics may present problems, but it also provides
a way,
To break them down, step by step, and find a perfect
solution each day,
It offers a unique perspective, with angles to view each
situation anew,
And a decimal point that teaches us to stay focused, and
see things through.

Mathematics also shows us that going round and round
may lead,
To the same point, time and again, while progress comes
from moving forward, with a steady speed,

It highlights the importance of mistakes, and learning
from them with care,
Inspecting and respecting errors, to grow and improve,
and show we're aware.

The exponential function teaches us to believe in higher
powers,
And that understanding is key, to reaching our goals,
and making our dreams devour,
Mathematics is not just numbers, formulas, and rules,
But a poetry of logical ideas, that help us make sense of
the world, and its many tools.
Like the set of numbers, a mother's love for her child is
endless,
And the universe, in all its vastness, is a mystery that's
still to be told,
Mathematics is simple, and so is life, when we see it from
the right perspective,
It's we who make things complicated, with our own
perceptions, and our own selective narrative.
Thank you, dear mathematics, for all that you teach,
A language of logic, and a way to understand, and reach.

28. What Is Science ?

Science is the systematic study of natural phenomena,
A quest for knowledge that drives us to ask questions
and explore.
It's an iterative process of experimentation and
discovery,
Where old methods are refined, and new ones are
employed.

Science demands a curious mind, one that investigates
and critiques,
A mindset that thinks critically, and perceives the world
with insight.
It's a journey of learning, unlearning, and relearning,
Where our understanding evolves, and our perspectives
are refined.

Science and spirituality, though distinct, complement
each other,
Both seeking truth, and a deeper understanding of the
world and its mysteries.

They intersect and inform one another, guiding us
toward a more profound comprehension,
Of the universe, and our place within it.

29. Don't Underestimate Her

Don't underestimate her strength, for she's a phoenix risen,
From the ashes of her past, she's reborn, with a spirit that's unbroken,
She's lifted herself, every time she fell,
And with each rise, she's become more resilient, and more powerful to compel.

She fought alone, but found the courage to heal,
To control her thoughts, and overcome her deepest fears, and reveal,
She shed her inhibitions, and let her true self shine,
With a fire burning within, that guides her, and makes her heart and soul align.

She's holding on to her dreams, with a determination that's strong,
And above all, she's chosen to be happy, and to live a life that's not wrong,

She's a woman of courage, with a heart that's pure and
bright,
And she'll rise above the challenges, and shine with all
her might.

30. It's Ok

It's okay to pause, and take a rest,
To slow down, and observe the small things, and be
blessed,
It's okay to feel lazy, and find a cozy spot to lie,
And let your guard down, and let your emotions dry.

It's okay to let go, of the things that weigh you down,
To maintain silence, and let your thoughts spin around,
It's okay to not react, to every situation and test,
And to take a step back, and let things unfold, and find
your best.

It's okay to travel, without a reason, or a plan,
To pamper yourself, at a coffee shop, and take a stand,
It's okay to sleep in, till late morning, once in a while,
And to enjoy your own company, in solitude, and let
your heart smile.

It's okay, to not be perfect, nobody is, it's true,

Accept your imperfections, and make peace with your
inner self, anew,
For in embracing your flaws, you'll find a sense of
freedom, and a heart that's light,
And you'll learn to love yourself, just as you are, and
shine with all your might.

31. Mother

'Mother' is the word that personify unending selfless
love.
She is the one draped in 6 yard
Sacrificing her happiness for her wards
With a big bindi on her forehead
Ready to face all hardship
Working untiringly from dawn to dusk
She is expert in house hold task
She has passed sleepless nights
She was the one who fought for our rights.
When I was weak, sick and ailing
She would sit by my cot without failing.
She would patiently pursue me to eat
So that I must stay fit.
She would see I got the best of everything.
A hug from her is most comforting touch in the world.
To the world you are my mother.
But for me you are the world!
Stay healthy and happy always, Mother.

32. Power Of Words

If you know the power of words
you will use them carefully
for a word from you
can makeup or cause breakup
in your relations.
For a hurting word spoken
Cannot be taken back.
Even if you want to take-up
The things ahead from here
it won't be possible to catch up again.
so think wisely to choose your words.
Wrong words can trigger a war.
Right words can bring peace.
That's the power of words.

33. Thinking Of You !

When I think of you,
I can smell your fragrance.
When I think of you,
There is a smile on my face.
When I think of you,
There are tears of joy in my eyes
For the good times we spent.
When I think of you,
I hear gentle breeze whispering into my ears.
When I think of you,
I can hear the song that you sang.
When I think of you,
My feet can feel the vibration of your dance.
When I think of you,
I can feel you by my side.
With you by my side, I can pass the toughest test.

34. A Mere Paper

A piece of paper one runs after,
If you don't have it enough
You try to own it faster.

It can get everything for you
But not happiness,
So its absence should not lead to unhappiness.

All are in a crazy race,
Forgetting relations in mad chase.

Fortunate ones have it in abundance
Without it, struggle for existence

If you have in plenty you get respect.
Without it, you have to introspect.

In its scarcity, your struggle is on for survival,
When in plenty, everyone waits for your arrival.

When in excess, it leads to fear
And if in scanty, it leads to tear.
Is it true my dear?

It is the cause of corruption,
When it is lost, causes depression.

For those who realise, less is more,
That's the time peace is restored.

Another paper most sought after
Not realising thereafter,
That it is a person's skill,
Which will create the thrill,
If it's getting too serious, just chill.

35. Be Yourself

Be proud of yourself for surviving,
the days which you felt most impossible, toughest n
darkest.
Be honest to yourself to accept your mistake,
accept the way you are and be real you.
Be kind to yourself to not feel guilty of the things,
you are unable to do.
Be happy with yourself for not changing
yourself to please people around you.
Be Happy, Be Yourself !

36. Welcome February

The last winter month
Chill out and last chance to flaunt your woollens.
It is also the shortest month of the year
It's a leap year with 29 days in February in 2024
So take the leap and grab the opportunities.

For those who have an affair with heavenly bodies
A good time of year to look up at the winter sky
In general a great time for star gazing
As less moisture in air during winter
Giving a clear view of the heaven.

For students the month of examination
But don't take tension
Give your hundred percent
And you will do the best.

For teachers a hectic month
Rushing to complete the syllabus,

Paper setting and paper correction etc.
List is endless but don't burn the midnight oil
Do remember to take rest.

For corporate and sales personnel
A month to complete the year ending targets.
Believe in yourself.
and you will meet the desired targets .
For women working or home makers
In every month they are planners, executors and
managers,
Multitasking to the best of their abilities.
Thus a happening month of the year.
So welcome dear February,
I am ready to take the challenges.
Face the challenges till challenges are not able to face
you !

37. Mosaic Of Her Life

Many a times she is broken into thousand pieces. Each time she broke, she handed over those pieces to God. For She had trust that God is always creative to put those pieces back and fix them in a new pattern like various colourful tiles or stones are put together by an artist to create a beautiful artwork. So what you see her today, is her new version All the beautiful pieces are put back together in more sassy, sparkling manner and the cracks prevailing all over allow more light to emanate through her very being. This is the mosaic of her life. Each fragment has its own story to tell. Each fragment adds a new dimension to her being. Each torn pieces were woven with utmost care. With loving hand HE has woven the tapestry from chaos to orderliness,from darkness to light from illness to healing,so that a new hope is born.

He has trusted her and given a brand new year ahead. She will definitely redefine her purpose of being on this planet before each pieces are turned into dust and lost forever. SHE is ME.

38. Power Of Positivity

The power of positivity, is so wonderful and bright,
A much needed spark that lights the darkest night.
It lifts the heart, it clears the way,
And turns the toughest ones to sunshine days.
With every thought, it builds a dream,
The power of light, a constant gleam.
It showers hope in times of doubt,
A voice that tells us we'll figure it out.
Like sun rays peeping through the rain,
Positivity helps us to rise again.
It's the ability to stand when we might fall,
A quiet courage that conquers all.
In every smile, in every word,
A healing power, that is often unheard.
For when we choose to think with grace,
The world becomes a better place.
So let your heart be filled with cheer,
For positivity is always dear.
In every challenge, every fight,
Positivity is our guiding light.

39. A Playful Cat

I just loved this white playful cat
when it came behind and sat
I was about to pat it
then it suddenly spotted a rat
went chasing behind it
on the way she saw another cat
prepared herself for the fight ,
It swelled up its fur and became fat
It climbed the nearby tree to defend itself
These animals never pretend themselves.
They can jump from the fence without making noise.
Enter the house through a window with poise.
An intelligent, sociable creature.

40. One Can..

One word can motivate a child
One mentor can make a difference in our life.
One lady can educate the whole family
One soldier can lead a country to victory
One flower can bring a smile to person in pain.
One song can lift up your mood.
One teacher can bring a change in students life.
One book can inspire whole generation.
One seed can start a forest.
One tree is a home to many.
One line can decide boundary of nations
One drop of water can give life.
One ship can save many from drowning.
One phone call can help someone live.
One ambulance can save many precious lives
One batsman can change the course of a cricket game
One corrupt politician can create unrest.
One right decision can change your life
One star can show direction to all.
One leader can change the nation.

One handshake can change the destiny.
One heart can know the truth
One beam of light can remove darkness.
One spark can create a fire to feed many.
One brick can lay foundation of whole building.
One electron can cause a chemical reaction.
One touch can heal the soul.
One friend is sufficient in times of need.
One mistake can put whole human race in danger
One virus can shake up the whole world.
My friends, so it's up to each one of you,
you are enough in yourself to bring the change
to make this world a better place !!!!

41. Inspire

Inspire with your story.
Infuse desire to excel.
Invigorate all with your presence.
In still compassion by your example.
Innovate methods to emerge as warriors.
and not to be just survivors

42. Love Puran Poli

A delicious traditional sweet dish - Puran poli
Is a part of every festival like Gudi padwa or Holi
Golden dough, stuffed with sweet delight,
Melt-in-the-mouth, a heavenly bite.

With jaggery and chana, the filling so pure,
Wrapped in a flatbread, soft and secure.
In each fold, a story untold,
Of memories shared and joys unfold

Amti on the side, with spices bold,
A tangy delight, its story told.
The mustard seeds dance, the curry so bright,
With tamarind's touch, it's love at first bite.

Puran poli with Amti, a feast so grand,
A tradition passed through each generation's hand
On this Guddi Padwa, with joy we say,
May blessings be yours on this festive day.

43. Modern Women

Women today are determined
They lead from the front.
Women today are fearless
They fight on the front
Women today are fit and agile
Taking the flight to greater heights
Women today are strong
Safe guarding the citizens of the nation.
Women today have precision and accuracy
Needed to launch space mission.
Women today are well educated imparting
Knowledge to future citizens of the nation.
Women today can express their ideas and can raise voice
against injustice.
she plays the role of daughter, mother, daughter in law,
sister in law all at same time.
She does all these by fulfilling her personal, family and
professional commitment.
Embrace her with love, empathy and respect as she is
standing tall in every situation.

Is she a human or a superhuman??

A human who is epitome of resilience, strength and multitasking.

Happy women's day!

(Note:This poem was published in TOI on Women's Day!)

44. New Year

Time for winter to chill.
Leaves turning from green to yellow and brown.
Time to turn the old to new.
Time to change the calendar on my wall
Time to change shorter days to longer days.
Time to look back at the year passing by
to reflect upon what I have gathered.
I realise that I gathered experiences good and bad
Grew wiser and stronger.
Gathered knowledge and created memories with loved
ones
Remembering the loved ones whom I lost.
Time to wrap up the year with a thank you note for
making me little more determined and little less
vulnerable.
And time to welcome the New Year!

45. Google Map Of Life

Some people and their advice are like Google maps in our life. If we take a wrong path with our Google maps working on our mobile, it quickly readjust our path from current location till the destination and tells the next turn we should take to reach our destination. It never says you are on wrong track and demotivates us. Thus we reach our destination sooner or later. Sometimes even if we don't reach the destination but at at least we get a new direction.

Similarly some people give us correct advice and shows us the new path to take when we become directionless or lost in life and they never discourage us by telling us that we can never reach our goal. Thus they help us to remain on track at least.

Value such people in life always.

46. A Question

A question posed, with words "good question" graced,
Can stir the mind, no thought left unchased.
But ask amiss, a path of error lies,
Where wrong begets the wrong, before your eyes.
Questions ignite, a curious inner flame,
To probe the unknown, and knowledge to claim.
Some seek the facts, the data hard and fast,
While others delve where meanings hold their cast.
Understanding's depth, a different quest,
To grasp the core, and truly be possessed.
And some arrive, a sudden, sharp demand,
To catch the slip, the thought not close at hand,
A mental jolt, to see if you're aware,
A fleeting test, hung lightly in the air.
Questions, the keys, to unlock what we seek.

47. My first Day Of School

The school gates swing, a brand new day,
A flutter of hearts in disarray.
With eager steps and curious eyes,
A fresh session beneath bright skies.
Who will be our class teacher, with gentle hand,
To guide our learning, helping to understand?
Our class teacher, yet unknown,
A seed of wonder newly sown.
Which room awaits, our learning nest,
And who will sit beside me near,
To share a laugh, to quell a fear?
My bench mate new, a friendly face,
To journey through this learning space.
So many questions, soft and low,
As seeds of hope begin to grow.
Welcome, dear students, brave and bright,
To fill these halls with joy and light.

48. You Went Without Goodbye

The space beside me fills the morning air,
Your silent absence makes a hollow sound.
You just went without goodbye, no last loving stare,
Just emptiness where warmth was always found.
A sudden severing, a painful merciless, swift tear,
You just slipped away, beyond my reaching hand.
This quiet heart now holds a haunting fear,
A life's unwritten, plans across the sand.
My heart, a broken vase upon the floor,
Holds only echoes of your gentle name.
This leaving, love, I can't fathom or soar,
My world devastated by a silent flame.

49. Moonlight In Full Moon

On a summer night, so soft and deep,
The full moon is capturing, its silver secrets keep.
A soothing breeze, a whisper through the trees,
Carries the fragrance of blossoms on the leas.
Moonlight is coming down as a pearly, tender grace,
Kissing the world with its ethereal face.
Two hearts entwined, beneath the lunar gleam,
Lost in a silent, captivating dream.
The air is still, save for the rustling leaves,
As love's soft magic silently weaves.
Bathed in the moon's romantic, gentle light,
This moonlit night, a memory glowing bright.

50. A Family

Though roots unseen, our lives entwine,
A family bond, a love so divine.
There no judging eyes, no envious glance,
In hearts of kin, always pure love dance.
Together we may sink or soar,
Through stormy seas or sunlit shore.
Whatever comes, we stand as one,
Our truest selves are known, not shunned.
Acceptance deep, a gentle art,
Forever held within the heart.
Through changing years and life's swift flight,
Our linked affections burn so bright.
A haven safe, a constant guide,
Where flaws are seen, but cast aside.
This precious bond, a gift untold,
A family's love, more worth than gold.